SNAKES
& OTHER
REPTILES
OF SOUTHERN AFRICA
A FIRST FIELD GUIDE

Happy birthday
Love from
Dogs and cats
x x

Page 54

Page 24

TRACEY HAWTHORNE

Contents

Page 28

Page 48

Southern African reptiles

Most people, when asked whether they like reptiles, will shudder and say either, 'Yuk! They're all cold and slimy!' or 'No way! They're poisonous!' In fact, the former is untrue and the latter applies to surprisingly few species in our region (see 'A note on venoms', page 8).

All reptiles have a dry, horny skin, usually modified into scales or plates. And, although they are 'cold-blooded', their blood may actually be just as warm as any other living creature's; the term 'cold-blooded' refers to the fact that all reptiles obtain their heat from external sources (usually the sun, which is why so many reptiles enjoy sun-bathing), unlike mammals and birds, which generate heat internally. 'Warm-blooded' creatures (like humans) need a constant supply of food to continually generate heat; some reptiles, on the other hand, can survive on as few as 10 meals a year.

Reptiles' ancestors were the early amphibians that crawled out of the seas about 370 million years ago; a group of these evolved into reptiles.

Page 52

In southern Africa today we have 480 species of reptiles, including the world's richest diversity of land tortoises. More than half are endemic[G]. Although only 46 of the most common reptiles have been included in this book, it is hoped that this selection will illustrate how interesting, resourceful and hardy – and, in many cases, beautiful – the reptilian life of southern Africa is, and encourage further investigation of this fascinating world.

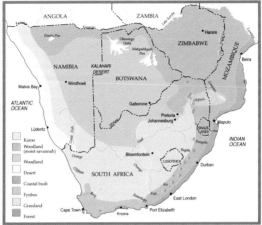

How to use this book

Each species' account is split up into several headings. These are explained below.

Common name: The 'common name' is the English name by which the reptile is known.

Scientific name: This is the official name by which it is known worldwide and is always written in *italic* type.

African names: Where possible, the reptile's name in Afrikaans (A), Xhosa (X) and Zulu (Z) has been supplied. (These are the most commonly spoken languages, after English, in South Africa.)

Length: Snakes, lizards, geckos, chameleons and crocodiles are all measured in a straight line along the backbone, from the tip of the snout to the tip of the tail. Only the shells of turtles, tortoises and terrapins are measured, along the midline of the carapace[G].

Use the ruler on the outside back cover to give you a realistic idea of the size of the reptile.

Identification: Characteristic physical features, colours and patterns (the parts of the different reptiles are illustrated on page 9).

Where found: The immediate environment preferred by the reptile (near water, for instance, or under loose leaf litter).

Page 26

The habitat map (on page 5) will give you an idea of the different types of vegetation found in the region, while the regional map (also on page 5) shows the South African provinces. These maps, used in conjunction with the distribution map that accompanies each species'

Page 11

account, will tell you where, geographically, the reptile occurs. The southern African region includes South Africa, Lesotho, Swaziland, Namibia, Botswana, Zimbabwe and Mozambique.

Habits: Different reptile have different social and feeding habits, and those with which you may not be familiar are marked with a ^G. A definition of these words is given on page 56, in the Glossary.

Reproduction: Short notes on egg laying and incubation periods.

Notes: Anything of special significance or interest.

Status: Whether the reptile is endemic^G, and protected, common or widespread. SA RDB 'Vulnerable' indicates that the reptile has been listed in the South African Red Data Book – a publication that lists all of our animals that are threatened with extinction.

Venom: Notes on type of venom, where relevant.

Food: What the reptile eats.

Similar species: Bear in mind that in many cases similar-looking species do not necessarily occur in the same location or habitat as the reptiles discussed in this book.

Reptiles

Indentifying reptiles

When identifying a reptile for the first time:

🦎. Take careful note of its general **shape**. Does it have legs or a long, smooth tail? Is the body fat and covered with spines? Note whether the head, body and tail differ in colour and pattern.

🦎. Look through this guide to find a photograph most closely resembling the specimen you have spotted, and check the **distribution** map to see if it has been recorded in your area.

🦎. Note the **habitat** in which it is living. Are you in a semi-desert region? Near a water hole or river? Is the animal sheltering under a rock or hiding in a tree?

Compare this with the notes under 'Where found'.

🦎. Observe the **behaviour** of the animal. Did it run up a tree or into a hole in the ground? Check against the notes under 'Habits'.

A note on venoms

Snakebites do occur, albeit rarely, and serious bites require treatment with antivenom. Cutting and sucking at a snakebite site or applying a too-tight tourniquet does not work and, in fact, may cause further damage. The best thing to do is to keep the victim calm and still, and get him or her to the nearest medical station as soon as possible. If you can do so safely, kill the snake and take it with you so it can be positively identified.

A note on reproduction

Most reptiles are oviparous (lay eggs), but some are viviparous (give birth to live young) and retain the eggs in the body for most or all of their development. These eggs hatch within weeks, days or even minutes of being laid.

Where to see reptiles

It takes patience to find reptiles: most are shy and scurry to safety at the first hint of danger. Look under boulders, rotting logs and grass piles; rubbish dumps are prime reptile habitats. Burrowing reptiles can be found by digging in loose soil under boulders and rotting logs. Check holes in the ground and stormwater drains that may act as pit-fall traps. In cooler regions, hibernating snakes and lizards can be found in old termite nests, and rock-living specimens in deep rock cracks.

When to see reptiles

Night searches often yield success: nocturnal[G] reptiles sometimes crawl onto still-warm roads at night, geckos collect around night lights where they feed on insects, and chameleons stand out against dark foliage in torchlight.

Early in the morning, before wind and the passing parade obliterate evidence, reptile trails can be followed in loose sand, particularly in spring, when the males are actively looking for mates.

Note: Most reptiles are protected by legislation, and permission must be obtained to collect them or their eggs.

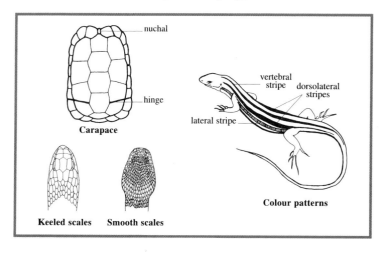

nuchal

hinge

Carapace

Keeled scales　　**Smooth scales**

vertebral stripe　dorsolateral stripes

lateral stripe

Colour patterns

Leopard Tortoise

Geochelone pardalis

African names: Bergskilpad (A); ufudu (Z).

Length: 30–45 cm; max. 70 cm.

Identification: Large. Domed, dark grey carapace[G], heavily blotched or streaked; some old adults have uniform dark grey-brown shell. Upper shell has no small scale (nuchal shield[G]) above neck; carapace not hinged[G].

Where found: Varied (montane grassland, fynbos, valley bushveld, arid and mesic savannah). Widespread, but absent from most of highveld, succulent Karoo and Namib Desert. Introduced to south-western Cape.

Habits: Occupies large home ranges (1–2 km^2).

Reproduction: Up to six clutches of six to 15 eggs each laid in summer; hatch 10–15 months later.

Notes: This is the biggest and most widely distributed land tortoise in the region.

Status: Widespread in suitable habitat.

Food: Plants, bones and hyaena faeces.

Similar species: Young could be confused with Bell's Hinged Tortoise.

Serrated or Kalahari Tent Tortoise

Psammobates oculiferus

African names: Kalahari- or skulprandskilpad (A).

Length: 8–12 cm; max. 14 cm.

Identification: Low, domed, light yellow-brown to dark brown carapace[G], patterned with yellow-brown stripes radiating from centre of each slightly raised scute[G]. Carapace lacks hinge[G]; has strongly serrated edge. Buttock tubercles[G] are present.

Where found: Dry savannah and scrub desert. Widely distributed in Kalahari and adjacent regions; absent south of the Orange River.

Habits: Burrows into loose soil at base of low shrub for protection.

Reproduction: Lays up to two eggs in a hole in spring or summer; hatchlings emerge in early autumn.

Notes: Although legal restrictions have been imposed, pet and tourist trades have decreased its numbers.

Status: Endemic[G].

Food: Small succulents and grasses; faeces.

Similar species: Geometric and Tent tortoises lack serrated edge to carapace[G].

Tent Tortoise

Psammobates tentorius

African names: Tentskilpad (A); ufudu (Z).

Length: 8–12 cm; max. 15 cm.

Identification: Small. Shapes and colours vary greatly; usually dark brown or black carapace[G] with geometric pattern of yellow or orange stripes. Carapace is not hinged[G], but may be domed or flat, with or without raised scutes[G]. Scutes along bridge broader than they are high. Has a nuchal shield[G].

Where found: Karoo, Western Cape and southern Namibia, in varied habitats, mainly dry, semi-desert regions.

Habits: Active in early morning and evening. Drinks by raising rear legs and sipping water that drains along shell grooves to forelimbs.

Reproduction: Up to three eggs laid in summer; these hatch after seven to eight months.

Notes: Males are much smaller than females.

Status: Endemic[G].

Food: Small succulents.

Similar species: Geometric Tortoise has scutes along bridge higher than they are broad; Serrated Tent Tortoise has spiny edge to shell.

Leatherback Turtle

Dermochelys coriacea

African names: Leerrugskilpad (A).

Length: 1,3–1,7 m.

Identification: A huge turtle weighing up to 800 kg. Black head and carapace[G], spotted with pale grey or blue. Carapace is rubbery, and has 12 prominent ridges. Head has pink or reddish mark on top. Underparts black, white and pink. Black tail. Long flippers.

Where found: Marine (tropical to temperate oceans), and beaches when nesting.

Habits: Lacks teeth; horny spines in throat enable it to swallow slippery prey.

Reproduction: Breeds on Maputaland beaches. Female lays six to nine clutches, each of up to 120 white, billiard-ball-sized eggs. Hatchlings emerge about 10 weeks later.

Notes: The heaviest living reptile.

Status: Endangered; SA RDB 'Vulnerable'.

Food: Jellyfish.

Similar species: Loggerhead Turtle is smaller, brown in colour, and has a flat, hard carapace[G].

Loggerhead Turtle

Caretta caretta

African names: Karetseeskilpad (A); ufudu lwasolwandle (Z).

Length: 70–100 cm.

Identification: Reddish-brown, smooth, elongate shell, tapering at rear. Neck, throat and sides of head yellow. Big, broad head with strong jaws. Two claws on each limb.

Where found: East coast. Marine (tropical to temperate oceans).

Habits: For first three years, drifts in surface waters foraging on softer foods; later hunts for hard-shelled prey in shallow coastal waters.

Reproduction: Breeds on Maputaland beaches. Female lays up to five clutches of about 100 eggs each.

These hatch after about two months.

Notes: Although entirely aquatic^G, comes to surface to breathe.

Status: Endangered; SA RDB 'Vulnerable'.

Food: Crabs, molluscs and sea urchins.

Similar species: Leatherback Turtle is larger and has prominent ridges on rubbery carapace^G; Olive Ridley Turtle has one claw on each limb.

Marsh or Helmeted Terrapin

Pelomedusa subrufa

African names: Moeras- or helmwaterskilpad (A); ufudu (Z).

Length: 20–30 cm.

Identification: Hard, very flat shell. Upperparts greyish-olive to blackish; underparts pale or blackish, with symmetrical markings. Two small, soft tentacles on chin.

Where found: Throughout; favours slow-moving and still water (pans, vleis, slow-moving rivers).

Habits: Withdraws neck sideways. Strong swimmer, but also basks on mud banks and travels briskly overland. In drier weather, digs into soil to await rains.

Reproduction: Following summer rains, female lays 10 to 30 soft-shelled eggs in sandbank. Hatchlings emerge about three months later.

Notes: Many are killed on roads when migrating to new vleis after rains.

Status: Very common in suitable habitat.

Food: Varied (omnivorous[G]): small birds, frogs, tadpoles, crabs, fish, waterweed and insects.

Similar species: None.

Peters' Thread Snake

Leptotyphlops scutifrons

African names: Peters se draadslang (A).

Length: 17–24 cm; max. 28 cm.

Identification: Very small and thin. Polished appearance. Red-brown to grey-black above; paler below. Blunt head. Eyes reduced to black spots beneath skin.

Where found: Grassland, coastal bush, mesic and arid savannah. In termitaria^G, under leaf litter and rotten logs, in northern regions; absent from Namib Desert and most of Cape.

Habits: Burrows. May sham death when threatened.

Reproduction: Female lays three to six elongate eggs, joined like a string of sausages, in summer.

Notes: The most common thread snake in the region.

Status: Common.

Venom: None.

Food: Ant and termite larvae.

Similar species: Western Thread Snake is more purplish in colour; Black Thread Snake is black; Cape Thread Snake has longer tail.

African Rock Python

Python sebae

African names: Afrika-rotsluislang (A); ugqoloma (X); umonya, imfundamo (Z).

Length: 4,25–5 m; max. 5,6 m.

Identification: Thick, muscular, body. Olive-coloured with dark blotches above; white with dark speckles below. Very small, smooth scales. Triangular head with large, dark spearhead mark.

Where found: In open savannah; on rocky outcrops and in bushveld near water; in northern regions, mainly in Lowveld.

Habits: Basks in sun and lies in water for lengthy periods. Hunts by ambush; bites into prey and then kills by suffocating it.

Reproduction: In summer, up to 100 orange-sized eggs laid in suitable cavity. These hatch about three months later.

Notes: Africa's largest snake. It has two heat-sensitive pits on upper lip, enabling it to detect body heat of prey and thus strike accurately even in the dark.

Status: SA RDB 'Vulnerable'.

Venom: None.

Food: Mammals (rock hyrax, steenbok, kudu calves), birds (pheasant, guineafowl), reptiles (crocodiles, monitors) and fish.

Similar species: None.

Cape Centipede Eater

Aparallactus capensis

African names: Kaapse honderd-pootvreter (A).

Length: 25–30 cm; max. 40 cm.

Identification: Small and slender. Coloration varies from grey-brown to red-buff; belly is cream; head is brownish. Small head has rounded snout and prominent black collar.

Where found: Varied habitats: highveld, montane grassland, savannah and coastal bush. Found among grass roots, and in leaf litter and disused termitaria^G in eastern regions.

Habits: Fossorial^G, living mainly in old termitaria^G, which provide shelter, warmth and food. Sometimes seen at night, particularly after summer rains.

Reproduction: Lays two to four eggs in summer.

Notes: When caught, struggles wildly and tries to bite; small teeth inflict little damage. Does not survive well in captivity.

Status: Common, but rarely seen.

Venom: Harmless.

Food: Centipedes.

Similar species: Reticulated Centipede Eater has dark body and two yellow collars on neck.

Common Brown Water Snake

Lycodonomorphus rufulus

African names: Bruin waterslang (A); izilenzi (X); ivuzamanzi elimdubu (Z).

Length: 60–80 cm; max 90 cm.

Identification: Slim, with small head. Plain olive-brown above; pale yellow-pink below. Small scales. Pink tongue.

Where found: In south and east, from Western Cape to Zimbabwe; moist situations (marshes, vleis, ponds and streams).

Habits: Mostly nocturnal[G]. Powerful constrictor. Excellent swimmer, can catch fish underwater; also takes fledglings (young birds unable to fly) from nests.

Reproduction: Lays six to 10 eggs in late summer; these hatch after about two months.

Notes: Tames easily and makes a good pet.

Status: Endemic[G].

Venom: None.

Food: Mainly small frogs.

Similar species: Dusky-bellied Water Snake has a dark belly band and a spotted upper lip.

Brown House Snake

Lamprophis fuliginosus

African names: Bruin huisslang (A); inkwakhwa, umzingandlu (X); inkwakhwa (Z).

Length: 50 cm–1 m; max. 1,5 m.

Identification: Muscular, smooth, shiny, rust-red body; obvious head has two thin yellow stripes on each side. Pale belly.

Where found: Varied habitats (highveld grassland to arid Karoo). Occurs throughout the region, around human habitation, under debris and stones.

Habits: Terrestrial[G]. Nocturnal[G].

Reproduction: Up to 20 eggs are laid; these hatch two to three months later.

Notes: This snake, one of the most common harmless snakes in the region, is useful in controlling pests. Often found around houses, hence its common name.

Status: Common.

Venom: None.

Food: Adults eat mainly mice and rats; juveniles eat lizards.

Similar species: Olive House Snake is plain olive-green.

Aurora House Snake

Lamprophis aurora

African names: Aurora-huisslang (A); inyoka (Z).

Length: 45–60 cm; max. 90 cm.

Identification: A pretty little snake: shiny green above, with prominent yellow-orange vertebral stripe. White below, sometimes edged with yellow.

Where found: Grasslands, coastal bush and fynbos. Occurs in moist situations and around human habitation in south and east, from Cape Town to Highveld.

Habits: Nocturnal[G]. Secretive and gentle. Constricts its prey.

Reproduction: Lays eight to 12 eggs in summer; these hatch after two to three months.

Notes: Frequently found near human habitation. Makes a good pet.

Status: Endemic[G].

Venom: None.

Food: Small rodents and lizards.

Similar species: Spotted House Snake is light brown with darker blotches; Striped Harlequin Snake also has yellow vertebral stripe but is darker and thinner.

Cape Wolf Snake

Lycophidion capense

African names: Kaapse wolfslang (A); inyoka (Z).

Length: 30–40 cm; max. 60 cm.

Identification: Uniform grey-black body, usually with white-tipped scales. Flattened head. Small eyes with vertical pupils.

Where found: Savannah and grassland. Widespread in east, under stones, logs and leaf litter, and in disused termitaria^G; prefers damp situations.

Habits: Nocturnal^G. Hibernates in termitaria^G, sometimes with other snakes, in winter. Kills its prey by biting then constricting it.

Reproduction: Lays three to eight eggs in summer.

Notes: The long, recurved (downward-curving) teeth of this snake give it its common name.

Status: Common; widely distributed.

Venom: None.

Food: Lizards (skinks); rarely eats small snakes.

Similar species: Variegated Wolf Snake is slender and has white mottling on back; Namibian Wolf Snake is dark brown above and has brown belly stripe.

Common Slug-Eater

Duberria lutrix

African names: Gewone slakvreter (A).

Length: 30–40 cm; max 43 cm.

Identification: Brick-red to pale brown above, sometimes with broken black vertebral line. Pale sides. Cream-coloured below. Stout-bodied, with smooth scales and small head indistinct from neck.

Where found: Savannah, coastal bush and fynbos; favours damp situations, such as under rock piles and on pond margins, in the south and east, from Cape Town to eastern Zimbabwe.

Habits: Snails are pulled out of their shells, often after an epic struggle. When threatened, ejects intestinal contents.

Reproduction: In summer, six to 12 live young born.

Notes: Inoffensive 'gardener's friend'. When handled, rolls up into a tight spiral.

Status: Very common in some areas.

Venom: None.

Food: Slugs, snails.

Similar species: Variegated Slug-eater is larger and has three rows of blackish spots on back.

Spotted Bush Snake

Philothamnus semivariegatus

African names: Gespikkelde bosslang (A); inyoka (Z).

Length: 80 cm–1 m; max. 1,2 m.

Identification: Slender-bodied, with flat, distinct, green or blue-green head and long bronze tail. Green body with dark blotches on forebody. Golden irises. Greenish-white to yellowish belly.

Where found: Savannah and thickets in north. Also occurs in open forest, extending into arid regions.

Habits: Mainly arboreal[G]. Accomplished, speedy climber, well camouflaged in foliage. Excellent vision. Actively hunts for prey among trees and bushes.

Reproduction: Lays three to 12 elongate eggs in summer.

Notes: In defence, inflates throat to show bright blue skin. Strikes and bites readily. Does not settle easily in captivity.

Status: Common in east, but very rare in southern Namibia and Namaqualand.

Venom: None.

Food: Lizards, geckos, tree frogs and chameleons.

Similar species: South-eastern Green Snake or Green Water Snake lacks blotching on forebody.

Common or Rhombic Egg-eater

Dasypeltis scabra

African names: Gewone eiervreter (A).

Length: 40–70 cm; max. 1,1 m.

Identification: Slender. Rough, keeled^G scales. Dirty-grey body with (usually) numerous blotches forming 'chequerboard' pattern. Prominent V-shaped mark on neck. Small, bluntly rounded head. Toothless mouth.

Where found: Throughout, in rock crevices and termite mounds. Occurs in varied habitats (absent only from true desert and forest).

Habits: Feeds in spring and summer; fasts in winter. Swallows eggs whole, but ejects collapsed shell.

Reproduction: Lays six to 25 eggs in late summer; these take two to three months to hatch.

Notes: Strikes readily. In defence, hisses by rubbing scales together and gapes wide, black mouth.

Status: Very common but rarely seen.

Venom: None.

Food: Birds' eggs.

Similar species: Brown Egg-eater is uniform brown in colour; Common or Rhombic Night Adder is stouter and has much bolder V-shaped marking.

Herald or Red-lipped Snake

Crotaphopeltis hotamboeia

African names: Rooilipslang (A); inyoka (Z).

Length: 50–75 cm; max. 80 cm.

Identification: Olive to green-black body, sometimes with white flecks. White to cream below. Obvious glossy black head, especially when freshly sloughed[G]. Large eyes. Bright red-orange lips (lips white or blackish in northern specimens).

Where found: Savannah and open woodland. Widespread in east, in marshy areas and around human habitation; absent from arid west.

Habits: Nocturnal[G]. Hunts in marshy areas. Prey is grabbed and bitten, and held until immobilised by venom. In defence, flattens head like viper and strikes.

Reproduction: Lays up to 15 eggs in early summer; these hatch about two months later.

Notes: Aggressive and quick to bite but tames easily. Bite bleeds freely but no toxic symptoms have been recorded in human beings.

Status: One of the most widespread snakes in Africa.

Venom: Harmless.

Food: Small frogs and toads; sometimes small lizards.

Similar species: Common or Rhombic Night Adder has bold V-shaped marking on top of head.

Eastern Tiger Snake

Telescopus semiannulatus

African names: Oostelike tierslang (A).

Length: 50–80 cm; max. 1 m.

Identification: Distinctive thin body and large, flattened head. Dull orange, with 22–50 dark blotchy bands, larger on forebody. Uniform yellowish to orange-pink below. Big, bulbous eyes with vertical pupils.

Where found: Savannah and sandveld; bushveld. On the ground, in trees and in rock crevices in north and east; absent from southern and eastern South Africa.

Habits: Nocturnal^G and mainly terrestrial^G; has been collected from trees. Slow-moving.

Reproduction: Lays six to 20 eggs in summer; these hatch in two to three months.

Notes:. Unpredictable and willing to bite.

Status: Uncommon and rarely seen.

Venom: Harmless to man.

Food: Small birds, bats, lizards and rodents.

Similar species: Namib Tiger Snake is sandy-buff; coral snake has narrow cross-bands encircling the body.

Boomslang

Dispholidus typus

African names: Boomslang (A); inambezulu, inyushu (X).

Length: 1–1,6 m; max. 2 m.

Identification: Variable coloration: male mottled black and gold or uniform bright green, red or powdery blue; female drab olive; juvenile twig-coloured, with bright emerald eyes and white or yellow throat. Scales slanting and strongly keeled[G]. Blunt head with diagnostic[G] very large eyes with round pupils.

Where found: In trees and shrubs; absent from dry west. Favours open bush and savannah.

Habits: Diurnal[G]. Arboreal[G], but readily leaves trees to move over open ground and will even cross water in pursuit of prey. Shy and elusive, but when threatened, inflates throat and bites.

Reproduction: Lays up to 25 eggs in summer; these hatch about three months later.

Notes: Locates prey with excellent vision. Highly venomous, but bites very rarely.

Status: One of the most widely distributed African snakes.

Venom: Potently haemotoxic[G], causing death from internal bleeding in one to five days.

Food: Agamas, geckos, chameleons, small birds and rodents.

Similar species: Green Mamba has smooth scales and smaller eyes.

Twig or Vine Snake

Thelotornis capensis

African names: Voël- or takslang (A); ukhokhothi (Z).

Length: 60 cm–1 m; max. 1,6 m.

Identification: Very thin, grey-brown body, with black and pink flecks and diagonal pale blotches, resembling twig. Lance-shaped head, variably coloured: uniform green or blue-green (in north-east), heavily speckled (in south-east) or with Y-shaped mark (in north). Large eyes with horizontal pupils.

Where found: Woodland from coastal forest to bushveld savannah.

Habits: Diurnal^G. Arboreal^G; perfectly camouflaged in trees; snake sways body in wind, appearing like a branch.

Reproduction: Female lays four to 18 elongate eggs in summer; these hatch about three months later.

Notes: One of few snakes that has the ability to see things in three dimensions, enabling snake to detect prey at a distance.

Status: A common but secretive snake in the northern savannahs.

Venom: Potently haemotoxic^G, may cause death from internal bleeding; fatal bites are, however, rare.

Food: Arboreal^G lizards, frogs, other snakes, fledgling birds and small mammals.

Similar species: None.

Spotted Harlequin Snake

Homoroselaps lacteus

African names: Gevlekte kousbandjie (A).

Length: 30–40 cm; max. 55 cm.

Identification: Small and slender. Brightly and variably coloured: black and yellow bands or blotches down body, with series of bright orange-red dorsal spots or orange-yellow dorsal stripe. Rounded, black head.

Where found: Varied habitats: semi-desert to savannah and coastal bush. Shelters in old termitaria[G] or under slabs of rock on sandy soils in south, central and eastern South Africa.

Habits: Fossorial[G]. Nocturnal[G]. Prowls in and out of grass tufts hunting for prey.

Reproduction: Lays six to nine eggs in summer. Hatchlings emerge after about 50 days.

Notes: Although mildly venomous, unlikely to bite because of its small gape.

Status: Common in some regions. Endemic[G].

Venom: Bite causes swelling, pain and headache, but is not fatal.

Food: Snakes, legless lizards (burrowing skinks).

Similar species: Striped Harlequin Snake is smaller and black with yellow dorsal stripe.

Coral Snake

Aspidelaps lubricus

African names: Koraalslang (A); inkamela (X).

Length: 40–70 cm; max. 80 cm.

Identification: Stocky, with broad head and large scale on nose. Boldly banded black and orange. Cream belly with black bands under neck.

Where found: Karroid and sandveld regions, dry valley plains. Rocky outcrops in arid western areas of the region.

Habits: Nocturnal[G]. Lives in underground burrows or under stones. Threatens by puffing and spreading a small, cobra-like hood.

Reproduction: Lays three to 11 eggs in summer; these hatch after about two months.

Notes: Hisses and lunges readily. Does well in captivity but seldom tames.

Status: Relatively common, but rarely seen.

Venom: Poorly studied; mildly neurotoxic[G], but rarely fatal.

Food: Small vertebrates (lizards and mice).

Similar species: Spotted Harlequin Snake and Eastern Tiger Snake are both slender and less regularly banded, and do not spread a hood.

Shield-nose Snake

Aspidelaps scutatus

African names: Skildneusslang (A); inyoka (Z).

Length: 45–55 cm; max. 70 cm.

Identification: Short, thickset, tan to pale grey-brown body, speckled with black. White below. Head and neck black; white eye stripe and throat band. 'Bulldozer'-like snout.

Where found: Savannah and sandveld. Under rock slabs, logs and leaf litter in north.

Notes: In defence may sham death. When threatened, rears and spreads a very narrow hood, and hisses.

Status: Endemic[G].

Venom: Mildly neurotoxic[G].

Food: Mice, frogs, small mammals, amphibians, lizards and other snakes.

Similar species: Coral Snake has reddish head marked with black, and is regularly banded on body.

Habits: Nocturnal[G]. Burrows in loose sand. May be seen on warm, wet evenings, foraging for prey.

Reproduction: Lays up to 12 eggs in summer.

Sundevall's Garter Snake

Elapsoidea sundevallii

African names: Sundevall se kousbandslang (A), inyoka (Z).

Length: 50–75 cm; max. 95 cm.

Identification: Stout, slate grey to black body, sometimes with a reddish or purplish sheen, and with pairs of dirty white rings along length. Yellowish or pinkish buff below. Smooth, glossy scales. Slightly pointed snout.

Where found: Under logs and rock slabs and in termitaria^G or deep sand, from central Namibia, east to southern Mozambique and KwaZulu-Natal. Occurs in a variety of habitats: grassland, coastal forest and sandy savannah.

Habits: Semi-fossorial^G. Nocturnal^G, although can be seen abroad in the late afternoon. Slow-moving.

Reproduction: Lays up to 10 small eggs.

Notes: Settles well in captivity.

Status: Endemic^G. Not very common.

Venom: Mildly toxic.

Food: Snakes, lizards and their eggs, frogs and small burrowing mammals.

Similar species: Boulenger's Garter Snake is smaller and has a more rounded snout.

Snouted Cobra

Naja annulifera

African names: Egiptiese or bosveldkobra (A); isikhotsholo (X); uphempethwane (Z).

Length: 1,5–2 m; max. 2,4 m.

Identification: Yellowish-brown, becoming blue-black with age, sometimes with yellowish-brown banding and a dark brown throat band. Thick body, very broad head. Smooth, dull body scales. Dull yellow below, with dark blotches.

Where found: Savannah and bushveld. In north and east of region, especially in Lowveld; often around human habitation.

Habits: Nocturnal[G], but sometimes sunbathes outside retreat early in morning. Shelters in disused termitaria[G], hollow logs and rocky outcrops. Rears and spreads broad hood; bites readily. Does not spit venom.

Reproduction: Lays eight to 30 large eggs in summer.

Notes: May become a pest in poultry runs.

Status: Widely distributed.

Venom: Potently neurotoxic[G].

Food: Small vertebrates (lizards, rodents, birds, birds' eggs and other snakes).

Similar species: Forest Cobra is brown on forebody, shiny black on rear half.

Cape Cobra

Naja nivea

African names: Kaapse kobra (A), koperkapel (A); isikhotsholo, umdlezinye (X); imfezi (Z).

Length: 1–1,5 m; max. 1,7 m.

Identification: Slender, with a broad head. Occurs in a variety of colours, from yellowish or brownish shades to purplish-black, but is always glossy in appearance.

Where found: Along river courses and around human habitation, mainly in drier south-western regions of South Africa, into Namibia and north into Botswana.

Habits: Shelters in burrows, and under rubble in built-up areas. Hunts by day and in early evening. When threatened, rears and spreads a broad hood, advancing on aggressor; bites readily. Does not spit venom.

Reproduction: Lays eight to 20 large eggs in summer.

Notes: This highly venomous snake sometimes enters houses in search of food and water.

Status: Common. Endemic[G].

Venom: Most potently neurotoxic[G] of all African cobras.

Food: Rodents, lizards, toads, other snakes, birds and birds' eggs.

Similar species: None.

Mozambique Spitting Cobra or M'fezi

Naja mossambica

African names: Mosambiekse spoegkobra (A); iphimpi (X); imfezi (Z).

Length: 1–1,2 m; max. 1,5 m.

Identification: Relatively small, with blunt head and smooth scales. Pink-grey to dark olive above, with black-edged scales; pinkish below, sometimes with dark crossbands or blotches on the throat.

Where found: Savannah and bushveld. In old termitaria^G, rodent holes and holes in walls, and around human habitation, in north and east.

Habits: Juveniles largely diurnal^G; adults mainly nocturnal^G.

Reproduction: Lays up to 22 eggs in summer.

Notes: Spits very accurately, aiming for upper body of attacker; also bites. Feeds well in captivity but rarely tames.

Status: Common in Lowveld.

Venom: Potently cytotoxic^G and neurotoxic^G; can cause partial blindness and skin loss.

Food: Toads; also other snakes, lizards, fledglings (young birds), rodents and grasshoppers.

Similar species: Western Barred Spitting Cobra has dark bands on grey-pink body; Black Spitting Cobra is bigger, and entirely black.

Rinkhals

Hemachatus haemachatus

African names: Rinkhals (A); inyoka emnyama (X); inyoka (Z).

Length: 1–1,2 m; max. 1,5 m.

Identification: Large and stout, with a wide head and one or two pale throat bands below. Coloration is varied; juveniles have about 40 black and tan bands, which persist into adulthood in some specimens in the east.

Where found: Grasslands; occurs in disused termitaria[G] and rodent holes, and around human habitation, in south and east of region.

Habits: Nocturnal[G]. Hunts in damp grassland. Shams death if threatened. Can rear and spit venom up to 2,5 metres; also bites.

Reproduction: About 30 live young born in summer.

Notes: Settles well in captivity, living for up to 11 years.

Status: Endemic[G].

Venom: Neurotoxic[G], potentially fatal in humans.

Food: Toads, mice, other snakes, lizards, birds and birds' eggs.

Similar species: Mole Snake does not spread hood; young Snouted Cobra has black band across throat.

Black Mamba

Dendroaspis polylepis

African names: Swartmamba (A); imamba (X); imamba emnyama (Z).

Length: 2,5–3 m; max. 4 m.

Identification: Largest venomous snake in Africa. Greyish-green, olive-green or grey-brown above; pale grey or grey-green below. Long, coffin-shaped head. Inside of mouth blackish.

Where found: Savannah; sub-tropical and tropical open bush. In holes in the ground, trees or rock crevices, in north and east. Often found around human habitation.

Habits: Terrestrial[G] and territorial[G]; emerges in early morning to hunt. Shy, but quick to rear, spread narrow hood, hiss and lunge repeatedly when under attack.

Reproduction: Female lays six to 14 large eggs in midsummer; hatch two to three months later.

Notes: Most infamous African snake; deserves respect.

Status: Widely distributed in eastern and southern Africa.

Venom: Very potent neurotoxin[G] and cardiotoxin[G], causing death.

Food: Rats, dassies, squirrels and small gamebirds.

Similar species: Snouted Cobra has dark brown bands across throat and spreads larger hood.

Common or Rhombic Night Adder

Causus rhombeatus

African names: Gewone or gevlekte nagadder (A); unomfuthwana (X); inhlangwana (Z).

Length: 30–60 cm; max. 1 m.

Identification: Short, muscular, grey-pink to olive-green body. Rounded head, usually with characteristic dark-brown 'V' across top. 20–30 dark, pale-edged, squarish blotches on back and tail. Grey to yellowish below.

Where found: In moist habitats in east and north, from Cape coast to Zimbabwe.

Habits: Nocturnal[G]. Eyesight poor; prey detected mainly by smell.

Reproduction: Up to 25 eggs laid in early summer; these take two to three months to hatch.

Notes: Huffs and strikes readily, but tames easily. Venom glands are large, but no fatalities have been recorded.

Status: Widely distributed in Africa.

Venom: Relatively mild, causing local swelling and glandular pain in humans.

Food: Amphibians (toads).

Similar species: Snouted Night Adder has pointed, upturned snout; Common or Rhombic Egg-eater is more slender and has keeled[G] scales.

Puff Adder

Bitis arietans

African names: Pofadder (A); iramba (X); ibululu (X, Z); ihobosha (Z).

Length: 60 cm–1 m; max. 1,2 m.

Identification: Large, thick, rough-scaled body, yellow-brown to light brown, with numerous dark, pale-edged chevrons. Some south-eastern specimens may be strikingly marked in orange or yellow and black. Broad, spade-shaped head with large, upward-facing nostrils. Pale below, with scattered blotches.

Where found: Throughout, from dry savannah to high-rainfall areas, except desert and mountain tops; common around farms.

Habits: Crepuscular[G] and sluggish. After striking, follows dying victim by tracking its scent with flickering tongue.

Reproduction: Up to 40 young born in late summer.

Notes: Most widely distributed venomous snake in Africa. Usually hisses before it bites.

Status: Common.

Venom: Potently cytotoxic[G], causing swelling and extreme pain, severe necrosis[G]; can be fatal.

Food: Small mammals; rodents, toads, lizards and birds.

Similar species: Berg adder is smaller and stouter and has more elongate head.

Berg Adder

Bitis atropos

African names: Bergadder (A); iramba lamatye (X).

Length: 35–50 cm; max. 60 cm.

Identification: Small and stout. Elongate head. Olive to dark brown above, with bold, elaborate blue-black and white-grey triangular pattern down back. Chin and throat pink or creamy, spotted with black. Dark arrow-head on crown. Dirty white to dark grey below.

Where found: Mountainous areas (plateaus, moist grassland and fynbos) from south-west to eastern Zimbabwe.

Habits: Ill-tempered, quick to hiss and strike. Ambushes prey. Often basks.

Reproduction: Up to 15 young born in autumn.

Notes: Rarely tames.

Status: Endemic[G].

Venom: Neurotoxic[G], causing loss of smell and taste and temporary blindness. Rarely fatal.

Food: Small rodents, amphibians, ground-nesting birds and lizards.

Similar species: Desert Mountain Adder has buff-grey back marked with dark and light bars; Horned Adder has single horn on ridge above each eye.

Cape Skink

Mabuya capensis

African names: Kaapse skink (A).

Length: 20–25 cm.

Identification: Very fat, shiny body. Stubby legs. Long tail. Light brown above, with three pale stripes down back and numerous dark crossbars.

Where found: Throughout, except in Namib Desert and extreme north and eastern regions; in burrows in loose sand, beneath rotting logs. Occurs in a variety of habitats including arid karroid veld, moist coastal bush and montane grassland.

Habits: Gentle and sluggish by nature, living on ground and hunting large insects in open spots.

Reproduction: Up to 18 young born in early summer; some females lay eggs.

Notes: Gentle by nature, this skink tames easily. Common around human habitation; is hunted by domestic cats.

Status: Common.

Food: Large insects (grasshoppers, beetles, crickets), spiders, worms.

Similar species: Western Three-striped Skink is thinner, boldly striped; Striped Skink lacks central stripe down back.

Variegated Skink

Mabuya variegata

African names:
Gespikkelde
skink (A).

Length: 10–15 cm.

Identification: Small and slender with long, tapering tail. Varied coloration. Usually light grey to dark brown above, with a speckled back and/or pair of pale stripes on sides. Has spiny scales on soles of feet; large eyes, with movable eyelids and a transparent window in each lower lid.

Where found: Throughout most of subcontinent; most common in Karoo and Kalahari. Occurs in a variety of habitats, including desert, karroid veld, montane grassland, savannah, coastal bush and valley bushveld.

Habits: Diurnal[G]. Seizes prey after short, fast dash from cover.

Reproduction: Breeding males develop reddish-brown blush below hind legs and on tail base. Females give birth to live young; small litters of up to four babies born in summer.

Status: Common and widespread.

Food: Spiders and beetles.

Similar species: Striped Skink is boldly striped with white or has numerous small pale spots; Variable Skink has bright white, dark-edged stripe on side.

Spotted Sand Lizard

Pedioplanis lineoocellata

African names: Gevlekte sandakkedis (A).

Length: 13–17 cm; max. 19 cm.

Identification: Slender body with long tail. Coloration is very varied, with some specimens being dull buff and others having bright colours. Adult usually has series of pale blue spots on flanks and spotted hind limbs; male may have blue-grey throat.

Where found: Karroid veld, valley bushveld, arid and mesic savannah. Also occurs in rocky flats and broken ground in south, west and central regions; absent from deep-sand areas.

Habits: Diurnal[G]. Quick, agile hunter, grabbing small insects after short dash from shaded cover.

Reproduction: Lays four to eight eggs in early summer; these hatch after about three months.

Notes: Lives as long as five years.

Status: Endemic[G].

Food: Small insects.

Similar species: Burchell's Sand Lizard is tan and brown and lacks spots on flanks.

Yellow-throated Plated Lizard

Gerrhosaurus flavigularis

African names: Geelkeel-pantserakkedis (A).

Length: 25–35 cm; max. 45 cm.

Identification: Small head, long tail. Body dark red-brown to olive, with two bright yellow, dark-edged stripes on sides.

Where found: Eastern regions, from Cape to Zimbabwe. Occurs in a variety of habitats, including montane grassland, savannah, bushveld, low and open coastal forest. Common in urban areas.

Habits: Shelters in burrow at base of bush or under boulder or rubbish. Quick and graceful, catches prey on the move.

Reproduction: Male develops bright red or light blue throat in breeding season. Up to six eggs laid in summer in small chamber dug in leaf litter.

Notes: Difficult to catch without causing tail to shed; nervous at first and bites readily, but tames easily and makes an interesting and long-lived pet.

Status: Very common.

Food: Grasshoppers, termites and millipedes.

Similar species: Kalahari Plated Lizard has speckled brown body and blue throat and flanks.

Rock or White-throated Monitor

Varanus albigularis

African names: Veldlikkewaan (A).

Length: 70 cm–1,1 m; max. 1,3 m.

Identification: Mottled tan and black. Dark streak running from above eye onto shoulder. Bulbous nose. Tail, banded yellowish-white and dark brown to black, is as long as body.

Where found: Savannah, arid karroid and semi-desert areas; also rocky grassland, open bush and forest country.

Habits: Lives in a tunnel, hole in a tree or a rock crack. Hibernates in winter. May sham death but bites readily in defence.

Reproduction: Lays 20 to 40 eggs in spring in hole dug in soft sand (rarely in live termite nest). These hatch after four months (in captivity) to a year (in wild).

Notes: Erroneously believed to drink milk from cows; in fact, it laps up water with its long, blue-and-yellow tongue. Rarely settles in captivity.

Status: Widespread; protected.

Food: Insects, millipedes, small mammals and reptiles (baby tortoises), birds and eggs, and snails.

Similar species: Nile Monitor is longer and slimmer.

Nile or Water Monitor

Varanus niloticus

African names:
Waterlikkewaan (A).

Length: 1–1,6 m; max. 2 m

Identification: Blotched black and yellow; juvenile brighter than adult, with bold yellow spots and cross stripes. Yellow below, with transverse grey-black markings. Elongate head. Laterally flattened, muscular tail, longer than body. Strong, stout legs.

Where found: Mainly in east, extending west along major waterways; also rivers, pans, dams, water holes and lakes.

Habits: Spends much time basking in sun at water's edge. Strong, swift swimmer, but also uses large claws to climb trees.

Reproduction: Lays up to 60 eggs in active termite nest in early summer; termites seal eggs inside; hatch six months to a year later.

Notes: The largest African lizard. Swims underwater to escape danger; when cornered, bites and lashes tail.

Status: Common along major waterways; protected.

Food: Crabs, frogs, fish, mussels, birds, crocodile and terrapin eggs and young.

Similar species: Rock monitor is shorter and stouter.

Southern Rock Agama

Agama atra

African names: Suidelike rots-koggelmander (A).

Length: 20–25 cm; max. 30 cm.

Identification: Blotched and mottled in brown and cream, with whitish streak running from neck to base of tail. Plump body covered with granules and scattered spines; crest along backbone. Broad head with rounded snout and wide mouth. Throat bluish. Top of head ultramarine in breeding males.

Where found: Rocky outcrops and boulders in south, from sea level to mountain tops, semi-desert to fynbos.

Habits: Forms colonies[G], sometimes quite dense, on rock outcrops, presided over by dominant male and female. Enjoys sun-basking. When threatened, flattens body against rock and fades bright head colours; may run off quickly.

Reproduction: Female lays two clutches of seven to 12 eggs each in summer. These hatch after about three months.

Notes: Preyed upon by rock kestrels.

Status: Endemic[G].

Food: Insects (ants and termites).

Similar species: Anchieta's Agama is smaller and has black-tipped scales on soles; Ground Agama male has less conspicuous blue head and three parallel black-ish lines on sides of throat.

Cape Dwarf Chameleon

Bradypodion pumilum

African names: Kaapse dwergver-kleurmannetjie (A).

Length: 13–16 cm; max. 18 cm.

Identification: Body leaf-green, usually with orange-red stripe on side. Head extends behind into scaly 'helmet'. Crest down spine and along upper half of tail, and on throat. Prehensile^G tail is longer than body.

Where found: South-western Cape; vleis, along river courses.

Habits: Can reach high densities in suitable areas, with up to six adults inhabiting a single bush. Catches insects with long, sticky, telescopic tongue.

Reproduction: Gives birth up to four times a year, between summer and autumn; up to 10 live young per litter.

Notes: Many chameleons are introduced with garden plants. They are not poisonous.

Status: Endemic.

Food: Insects (small grasshoppers).

Similar species: Dwarf Chameleons all look very similar, but the many species are rarely found together.

Flap-neck Chameleon

Chamaeleo dilepis

African names: Flapnekverkleurmannetjie (A).

Length: 20–25 cm; max. 35 cm.

Identification: Large. Coloration varies from pale yellow and salmon-pink to greens and browns; sometimes speckled. Usually pale stripe down side of body and two pale spots on each shoulder. Skin flaps behind head.

Where found: Savannah woodland and coastal forest in northern, central and eastern regions.

Habits: In defence, male inflates neck to show bright orange interstitial[G] skin, gapes mouth to reveal orange lining, flattens body, rocks from side to side and hisses menacingly.

Reproduction: Lays about 50 small eggs in late summer; these hatch five to 10 months later.

Notes: Easiest to find at night, when it turns blue-white in colour. Is not poisonous.

Status: Common in suitable habitat.

Food: Flying insects (beetles and grasshoppers), spiders, snails and centipedes.

Similar species: Namaqua Chameleon has crest of knob-like tubercles[G] along spine.

Moreau's Tropical House Gecko

Hemidactylus mabouia

African names: Moreau se tropiese huisgeitjie (A).

Length: 12–16 cm; max. 17 cm.

Identification: Light grey to greyish-brown above, sometimes with four to five faint, dark crossbands. Cream-coloured belly. Tail has 10–12 dark bars. Flat head and large eyes with vertical pupils.

Where found: Mainly in east, in varied habitats (arid and mesic savannah and coastal bush); frequently enters homes.

Habits: Arboreal[G] and nocturnal[G]. Males are territorial[G] and fight furiously. Often attracted by house lights in Lowveld.

Reproduction: One or two hard-shelled eggs are laid (sometimes communally, in batches of up to 60).

Notes: Makes a 'tik-tik-tik' sound.

Status: Common in northern parts of region, and expanding in south.

Food: Moths, beetles and cockroaches; larger specimens take small lizards.

Similar species: Can be confused with Tasmin's House Gecko.

Bibron's Thick-toed Gecko

Pachydactylus bibronii

African names: Bibron se geitjie (A).

Length: 15–20 cm.

Identification: Large. Greyish or purplish-grey to brown back with white spots and four to five indistinct, dark crossbands. Rough skin with numerous keeled[G] tubercles[G]. Tail segmented with whorls of spiny scales. Triangular head with powerful jaws.

Where found: Occurs in varied habitats, from karroid veld, semi-desert, to arid and mesic savannah. Among rocks, in houses, and under loose stones.

Habits: Gregarious[G], form-ing large colonies[G]. Adhesive discs on toes enable it to climb up walls. In defence, readily sheds tail.

Reproduction: Lays two eggs in hole or crevice.

Notes: One of the most common geckos. Its bite can be painful, but is not poisonous. Although aggressive, makes a good pet.

Status: Widespread.

Food: Insects and smaller lizards.

Similar species: Spotted Gecko is smaller; Marico Gecko is smooth, slender and thin-legged.

Nile Crocodile

Crocodylus niloticus

African names: Nylkrokodil (A); uhlobo oluthile icngwenya (Z).

Length: 2,5–3,5 m; max. 5,9 m.

Identification: Unmistakable. Large (weighing up to 600 kg) and heavily armoured with horny plates. Long jaws with prominent teeth. Webbed hindfeet. Eyes and valved nostrils on top of head.

Where found: Rivers, lakes, water holes, swamps and estuaries, in north and east.

Habits: Amphibious^G, basking in sun during day and sheltering in water at night. Young eat insects and frogs, while adults ambush larger prey.

Reproduction: Lays 20 to 80 eggs in hole dug in sandbank.

Female guards nest. About three months later, hatchlings peep to alert mother, who digs open nest to release babies.

Notes: Attacks on humans, and fatalities, have been recorded. Nowadays, confined largely to game reserves; hunting has reduced numbers in the wild.

Status: SA RDB 'Vulnerable'.

Food: Frogs, mammals (antelope, zebra), birds, fish and carrion.

Similar species: None.

Glossary

Amphibious: Living both on land and in water.

Aquatic: Living in water.

Arboreal: Living in or among trees.

Carapace: Upper section of tortoise, terrapin or turtle shell.

Cardiotoxin: Poison that attacks function of the heart.

Colonies: Associating in close proximity when sheltering, feeding or breeding.

Cytotoxic: Poison that attacks cells and tissues.

Crepuscular: Active at twilight or just before dawn.

Diagnostic: Conclusively aiding in identifying a given reptile (a reptile that has a 'diagnostic' feature can be identified by that feature).

Diurnal: Active during the day.

Endemic: A species whose range is confined to one region.

Fossorial: Living underground.

Gregarious: Living together in groups.

Haemotoxic: Poison that affects the blood.

Hinged: Referring to the flexible joint in the shell of some tortoises that allows the front or rear of the shell to close.

Interstitial: Referring to the skin between the scales.

Keeled: Prominently ridged, referring to the backs of some geckos and the dorsal scales of some snakes.

Necrosis: Death of body tissue, usually due to an interruption of the blood supply to that part.

Neurotoxic: Poison that interferes with the nervous system and causes it to malfunction.

Nocturnal: Active at night.

Nuchal shield: Enlarged scale at front of carapace.

Omnivorous: Eating any type of food.

Prehensile: Adapted for grasping, especially by wrapping around a support.

Scute: Enlarged scale.

Sloughed: Shed; usually referring to the dead outer layer of a snake's skin.

Termitaria: The nest of a termite colony.

Terrestrial: Adapted to living on the ground.

Territorial: Referring to the behaviour of a reptile that establishes and then defends a territory against others.

Tubercles: Small, rounded protuberances.

Photographic credits

W R Branch: front cover (right, top and bottom), pg 1 (right), 6, 7, 14, 16, 22, 25, 26, 27, 29, 31, 32, 33, 34, 35, 36, 40, 41, 43, 44, 45, 50, 53, 54 back cover (top and bottom); **Roger de la Harpe:** pg 13 (SIL); **Nigel J Dennis:** front cover (left), pg 37, 52; **Leonard Hoffman:** front cover (deep etch), pg 2, 12 (SIL), 15 (SIL) 17–20 (SIL), 23, 24, 28, 30 (SIL), 38 (SIL), 46 (SIL), 47 (SIL), 51 (SIL); **A Pauw:** pg 3, 48; **Peter Pickford:** pg 49 (SIL); **A J Stevens:** pg 1 (left), 21, 39, 42; **Philip van den Berg:** pg 4; **John Visser:** pg 10, 55.
SIL = Struik Image Library